Songs of the Underland

& Other Macabre Machinations

Kurt Newton

Songs of the Underland & Other Macabre Machinations

This book is for Amy

who brought me out of the
Underland

FOREWORD

FOREWORD **13**

SONGS OF THE UNDERLAND 19

As the Dream Descends 21

The Underland 23

The Balance of the World 25

The Song of the Underland 26

The Resurrection of Love Beyond 27

The Man with No Name 29

The Mercurial Clouds of Misery 32

The Church of the Unholy Choir 34

The Head of the Priest of Contemptible Lies 37

In the Dens of Unending Equity 38

A Dream of Love Unadorned 40

The Wanderers 41

The Scarlet Penance 43

Titus Healing 46

The Great and the Small 49

The Chair of Absolution 51

The Mimic 53

Where the Sun Shines Never 56

The Twin Cities 58

Inside the Walls of the City that Never Sleeps 61

OTHER MACABRE MACHINATIONS.. 65

The Underwater Circus 67

The Cottage on the Lake 70

Phantastikon 72

The Fetch 73

The Malingering 74

The Soul that Knew No Solace............... 77

Funeral for Annette 79

Bone Riders... 83

The Promise of Eternity 84

The Crows of Las Cruces.......................... 87

The Crows of Las Cruces Revisited 91

The Black Star Traveling Show................. 95

Dancing in the Dark................................. 96

The Suckling.. 98

Redcap.. 103

Whispers Beyond the Glass 104

Beyond the Blue Veil................................ 107

The Memory of Persistence 110

The Illustrations of Robert Ingram Price.............. 112

Outside These Chamber Walls............................ 115

A Pen and a Promise to Keep 117

His Horror's Masterful Voice.................................. 118

ACKNOWLEDGEMENTS 121

AFTERWORD 125

KURT NEWTON 127

THE RAVENS QUOTH PRESS 129

Foreword

Entertaining the Dark
The Inception of *Songs of the Underland*

Why do I write what I write?

I t's a common question that people ask me. It's a question I often ask myself—especially when the written work is disturbing. It isn't often I set out to write about a particular subject matter knowing where it will lead. The thrill I receive from writing is in the exploration of thoughts and actions and the

consequences those thoughts and actions might bring. A lot of what I write is cautionary. *What if* scenarios abound. Sometimes that *what if* is enough to explore an entire landscape of ideas. As was the case with *Songs of the Underland*.

Songs of the Underland began as two poems: "The Underland" and "The Resurrection of Love Beyond." Here are the two poems in their original incarnations:

The Underland

It is a place where nightmares dwell,

where untethered shadows live and breathe,

beneath the pavement of reality lies

a hellish world that one should never hope to see.

To get there all one has to do is fall,

the rabbit hole is never what it seems,

one slip and not a soul will hear you

calling as you disappear just like a dream.

Once there you'll find yourself at home,

in the shadow of your former self,

a state of being where kindness has left

your bones and been replaced by something else.

The principles you compromised,

the choices made throughout the years—

all will knit together to form a pleasant

disguise to mask the growing fear.

For it's too late to do what's right,

as your former self will naggingly attest,

in every reflective surface your withered soul

will wave goodbye to the life you once possessed.

Because once you've crossed into the Underland,

there is no end to the weight that you must bear,

you'll spend all your tomorrows just trying

to understand the fate that brought you there.

~

The Resurrection of Love Beyond

Thoughts of you and your luminous face

cast a light where nightmares hide and shadows dwell,

it unchills my blood and fills this darkened space,

as I endeavor to one day depart this infernal realm.

This world I now inhabit is but an arduous maze,

my search has yielded intricate layers ever-deep,

and still at every turn I hope to find my way

back to the one true thing my previous life bestowed to me.

This labyrinth is designed to obfuscate,

to feed upon the weakness of a weary soul,

but during my search I've begun to excavate

the pieces hidden that have hindered me from being whole.

So, I beg of you, my dear, your eternal patience while you wait,

as one by one I reassemble my scattered bones,

I promise you, what mortality deemed to separate

our love will resurrect and bring me home.

~

Both poems describe a nether world of nightmare and shadow where a kind of spiritual penance is meted out. These original versions are much different than the versions that eventually became part of *Songs of the Underland*. Both were weak in their execution. But, in both, were the seeds of the world I would later explore. The problem with the original poems was they were too distant, too much like a tourist snapping photographs. I needed to make them personal. I needed to put myself in this hellish landscape of sin and forgiveness if I was going to return with something worthwhile, something redeeming. So I mined the hellish landscape of divorce.

I don't talk much about my divorce from my first wife, if at all. But, as anyone who has been through the process, a divorce just doesn't involve a spouse. It often times involves children. A house. Even pets. It's the dissolution of a family. All of this was true in my case. After a long marriage, I was the one who initiated the breakup.

This was many years ago. I've since remarried and am much happier as a result. But the old wounds are still tender; the old guilt still as fresh when scraping back the surface. While writing *Songs of the Underland* I'm sure I tapped into the purgatory that still exists in my subconscious when it comes to the reasons why my divorce happened, and the damage done. Although there was no physical abuse, there was harm to the psyches of everyone involved, I'm sure. Song is just another word for regret, and Underland another word for guilt.

So, *Songs of the Underland* is truly a cautionary tale. One

where personal ambition supersedes love, where the quest for the material supersedes the spiritual, and the damages that accrue.

Each of us has our own set of dark songs we keep to ourselves.

May your dark songs be few.

Kurt Newton

Woodstock Valley, CT

20 March 2022

SONGS OF THE UNDERLAND

KURT NEWTON

As the Dream Descends

As the dream descends, my body deflates,
chest and torso sink into the mattress;
I slip down into the Underland,
where unnamed creatures lie in wait,
their faces white and featureless,
in chambers cold and damp.

What follows next is always the same,
I navigate the catacombs in fear that death
will extend its cold, white hand
and stop me before I can escape.
But then the morning sun fills my head,
and I rise a free and thankful man.

I once believed that dreams were safe,
playgrounds of imaginative excess
that ease the mind of the day's demands.
But what follows me when I wake,
is a feeling of unspeakable duress,
as if pursued by something damned.

This horror is due to the pact I made,
a youthful indiscretion I must confess,
with forces I did not fully understand:
my theoretical soul in exchange
for a life of supreme success;
the outcome of which I surely did not plan.

Imagine my surprise when every day
good fortune rained at my behest,
and soon I was richer than the richest man.
I knew then the debt I'd have to pay
would be my soul and nothing less,
and so the dreams began.

And here I am, as once again I brace
for the inevitable nightly harness
that lowers me amid those who hold command.
For I know if I should lose my way,
the sun won't rise and I'll be left bereft,
another unnamed creature of the Underland.

The Underland

For you, my friend, it's not too late,
these words are like a message in a bottle thrown
to those who fail to contemplate and understand
there is a place beyond the pale of what is known;
that place is called the Underland.

It is a hellish world of dirt and stone,
a dimlit place where grotesque creatures thrive
in dampened chambers fed by luminescent streams
of fetid waters that swirl and seethe as if alive;
a place that should most surely haunt your dreams.

I cannot stress enough the wisdom I've derived,
the consequence of each and every choice one makes,
the lesson not to tread where hatred dwells,
not to wallow in the pointless pain of past mistakes,
or one will find oneself alone in a living hell.

For me, my friend, it was much too late,
I was selfish with the riches I received,
and to love another I had neither time nor care,
and so one night, in a drunken stupor, the air appeared to cleave,
and I tumbled down a spiral stair.

I awoke in a place I could not leave
among the ruins of some former denizen,
there a hideous transformation took hold,
my skin began to twist, my bones to bend,
to match in appearance the corruption of my soul.

So let this be a warning, my dear friend,
who might assume nothing will come of your neglect,
who believes a clean conscience is achieved by clean hands,
a far worse fate than disease or death
awaits you in the Underland.

The Balance
of the World

There will come a day
when the balance of the world will tip
in favor of the damned,
the ground will heave, the earth will split
and up will rise a seething tide
of denizens from the Underland.

But just like those
who occupy this cherished life
and work at every turn to save their soul,
a similar battle wages deep beneath, a fight
for dignity, a fight by those displaced
to find their way back home.

So there may come a day
when the balance of the world will tip
in favor of the saved,
a battle not foretold by any ancient manuscript,
where dreams ascend, redeeming men
who have simply lost their way.

The Song
of the Underland

In the memory cathedrals
where silence has no home,
a discordant melancholia regales
from organ pipes of stone.

A sinfonia of shattered dreams
that grips the psyche in its hands,
and squeezes till a tortured scream
sings the Song of the Underland.

A timpani of tattered things
that beat against the chamber walls,
a futile ululation echoing
the music's rise and fall.

A ghastly composition heard
only by the damned,
every day from this day forward:
the Song of the Underland.

The Resurrection of Love Beyond

Thoughts of you and your luminous face
casts a hopeful light where nightmares hide and shadows dwell,
it unchills my blood and fills this darkened space,
as I endeavor to one day find my way out of this living hell.

I must admit, the choices made throughout my life,
the principles I compromised, are damnable—there's no defense,
and yet, there is no place in this infernal realm I now reside
for a love so pure, a love my ghost-filled heart believes
deserves a second chance.

And so I search the endless catacombs,
entering forbidden chambers where creatures guard the
remnants of their hosts,
I venture deep where one should never seek to roam
in an attempt to find the scattered pieces of my long-forgotten soul.

So, I beg of you, my dear, your eternal patience while you wait,
as one by one I reassemble the parts of me that
      once upon a time were whole,
I promise you, what mortality deemed to separate
our love will resurrect and at long last bring me home.

The Man with No Name

I met a man who had no name,
whose face was frozen in a rigor
that displayed his final shock,
before the balance in his soul was tipped
and he became another wanderer amid
the luminescent streams and crumbling rock.

His name was lost, identity stripped,
like all of us here, remanded like unruly children
sent to their room to think about what they've done,
but he was the first poor soul I partnered with
to understand this strange new world
and the ugly creatures we'd become.

He led me to a secret place
where those who came before
with hobbled hand had left their mark.
A roadmap of sorts etched in stone
to show the way toward some dark unknown?
Or was it madness in the form of art?

He allowed his body to be scribed,
so I dug my fingernails into his back
and traced the map upon the canvas of his skin,
and from there we began a quest for answers,
answers we had hoped to find before
our hideous cancers deformed us from within.

The catacombs were in fact
a serpentine pattern of entry points
all leading to one central core,
like a bloodshot eye or a purple bruise,
its veins radiating like a tentacled beast
asleep on the ocean floor.

Together we walked for days it seemed,
encountering creature after creature
each more hideous than the one before,
until we saw ahead in the mist
a great walled city that loomed like a ship
lost on the forgotten seas of ancient lore.

I turned to the man who had no name,
elated we had reached our destination,
that the map upon his back had held true,
but he had lagged behind with ragged breath,
and in one last act of kindness
he told me what I must do.

"Run!" he growled,

his throat constricted, his twisted limbs

dragging in the dirt as he advanced,

and I ran toward the doors and pounded

until a slide window opened

and an eye pierced me like a lance.

"What is it you seek?"

a voice spoke from beneath the eye

on the obverse of this massive door.

The man with no name was no longer a man

but a machine of death sheathed in cursed flesh:

"Redemption!" I implored.

They let me in and so here I am

in the company of strangers

more stranger than any I'd every hoped to meet,

congregating with the lost

while navigating the hallowed halls

of the City That Never Sleeps.

The Mercurial Clouds
of Misery

The city was a vast favela
of makeshift hovels and squatters' pits
constructed of rock and dirt and bone.
Everywhere there were candles lit,
candles made of earwax and the oily pus
that oozed from wounded souls.

The candles sent an acrid smoke
into the air that hung like a cloud above,
a cloud that behaved with a life of its own,
a malevolent ever-present judge,
writhing and roiling with the tormented faces
of those to which we should atone.

These mercurial clouds were omniscient,
the faces different for each set of eyes
that chose to cast their gaze.
It was a haunting conjured by lies,
a ghostly remnant of guilt intended
to expose our wicked ways.

The madness it produced
was too great a pain for some,
and for others an annoyance at best.
I fell into the former, stricken dumb,
my heart a crazed animal
thumping wildly in my chest.

I ran through the narrow alleyways
that separated the hovels from the pits,
the clouds swimming in my brain
like a drug I could not resist,
a drug that offered only
the untold misery of the insane.

And then the clouds were gone,
the faces once again hidden deep,
replaced by strangers fueled by fire.
A mournful music stirred my sleep
and awake I lurched inside
the Church of the Unholy Choir.

The Church of
the Unholy Choir

It took some time to understand the Underland
and who or what was at its helm.
The dead were not eternally damned
and could find salvation in this realm.

Redemption in the form of penance
was a promise for every soul.
But there were factions here who believed
to be redeemed was not a virtue to extol.

The largest of this group was a flock of followers
who worshipped every form of sin,
in a great smoky amphitheater
where blood was thick and trust was thin.

One day I found myself wandering in an abject
delirium and they promptly took me in.
They cleaned me up and clothed me,
they fed me sorrows and sang me hymns.

The first thing I noticed was a mournful music
that only cold caverns and lonely grottoes could inspire,
music not of the remorseful or the repentant
but of the Church of the Unholy Choir.

The Priest of Contemptible Lies
presided over our daily mass.
He spit and spewed a litany of evils
he said would surely come to pass.

He puffed and pointed from his pulpit
across the sea of sufferers of moral thirst.
The Underland would not be saved, he claimed,
until each of us did our worst.

Become the demon, the denizen,
the creature for which you were made!
For when there are enough of us,
the scales will be outweighed!

We will spill into the world above
and take out rightful place!
And once again all God's men
will bear witness to his true face!

And so I began to weigh the scales
that tipped within my soul,
sing the Church's praises of sin?
Or seek the truth that would make me whole?

Under cover of smoke I fell from grace
and slipped beyond the thousand eyes,
I left the amphitheater with the head
of the Priest of Contemptible Lies.

Of course, another will take his place,
perhaps worse than the one before,
but I did my part, a good deed done
toward evening the score.

The Head of the Priest of Contemptible Lies

Here lies the head of the Priest of Contemptible Lies,
a gag stuffed in its still-preaching mouth,
coins placed on its eyes to keep it blind,
buried deep in the catacombs where it cannot be found.

But nothing here remains lost forever,
and nothing here ever dies.
There will come a day when the body from which it was severed
will reunite with the head of the Priest of Contemptible Lies.

And when that day comes I hope to be gone,
free from the Underland and the horrors it breeds,
free to dream happily in the great beyond,
free even from what it means to be free.

In the Dens of

Unending Equity

For some time I remained hidden
in the farthest reaches of what was known to be
the final resting places of the unredeemed,
men in full transformation
in the Dens of Unending Equity.

This was the last stop
for many a man who forfeited the dream,
in caverns dark far from any luminescent stream,
their bodies in full rejection
of any semblance of humanity.

Abominations unimaginable
that were never meant to be,
a slithering, quivering mass of appendages and gnashing teeth,
sounds so hideous I wished I could unhear
the songs of sickness they sang to me.

And though I could have been eaten
by any number of creatures I could not see,
it was here I found solace in the cloak of anonymity,
a cloak I knew I'd have to burn
upon my return to the City That Never Sleeps.

And so I humbly rehearse my alibi
among these cursed monstrosities,
a future glimpse, or worse, if I do not heed
the lessons found upon these unholy grounds
in the Dens of Unending Equity.

A Dream of Love Unadorned

I dream a dream of love unadorned,
untampered, untethered, unmeasured, unworn.
Such a treasure this love, to be shared and not borne
out of fear of being alone.

I dream a dream of love that is true,
a quiet dream that in my heart once grew,
a dream I let die on the vine in vain pursuit,
forsaking family and home.

I dream a dream of love everlasting,
beyond wills, beyond words, beyond each other's passing,
a dream I once had but deemed not worth having—
for this, I will atone.

The Wanderers

In between caverns and nooks and dens,
where the grotesque grovel and the hideous host,
there are miles upon miles of catacomb with no end
where there are wanderers who wander like ghosts.

They appear as barely perceived spirits or wraiths
as they dart and then disappear from view,
leaving you adrift and tossed between fates
with no care for what happens to you.

These are no ordinary men of lost virtue and lost pride,
they are intentional in their unbound pursuits,
they think themselves superior with quick mind and keen eye,
that for every puzzle they face there's a way through.

I was one such wanderer when I first arrived in this place,
in this god-forsaken maze of the Underland,
and then by chance I happened upon the Man with No Name
and let my direction be guided by his hand.

For the first step for any wanderer lost
to find his way to the City That Never Sleeps
is to listen to the message hidden in the song
given to every man and every beast.

But some, no matter what, will always find a way
to wander and remain wanderers for life,
lost in the ruins of all they survey
unfriendly ghosts in an unending night.

The Scarlet Penance

Once back inside the City That Never Sleeps,
it wasn't long before my judgment hour.
I kept myself away from prying eyes
and still my face was recognized,
and I was dragged gagged and bound
to the Church of the Unholy Choir.

A new priest had commandeered the sound
from the throats of a thousand soulless men,
and today I was to be availed
to pay the cost for my betrayal,
with sharpened blade and ruthless strike
across the trembling surface of my chest.

The bladesman was skilled in both depth and site,
a surgeon in a previous life, no doubt.
The muscles of my chest were splayed,
my heart exposed inside its cage
like a frightened bird that beat its wings
in a futile effort to fly about.

It was then the choir began to sing,
a song so painful it squeezed my heart.
The wound was like a gaping maw,
a scarlet penance I could not ignore.
I was dumped outside and left to weep,
my body stripped and torn apart.

I dragged myself into the dark to keep
from prying eyes and soulless laughter.
Death will not come, do not fear.
Death no longer knows you're here.
A voice as hideous as any monstrous face
wormed into my ear shortly thereafter.

I know a man, the voice went on to say,
who can take a wound of any size,
and make it smaller than a speck.
Would you like for me to fetch him quick?
His name is Titus Healing, isn't that a hoot?
Just say the word and he'll arrive...

I must have agreed, for when I came to,
a man no larger than a child
had made a poultice of turmeric,
it could have been rust mixed with spit
for all I knew,
but the pain began to wane inside.

But the poultice was mere substitute
for the heart that once beat in my chest.
When I realized my condition,
the man-child healer was missing,
my heart in his possession
still beating with the love for the one I left.

Titus Healing

I made my appeal to the only one present.

"A deal's a deal," the voice said.

"Show yourself," I called,

and out from the shadows a creature crawled.

"I need it back!" I pled.

The creature laughed and shook its head.

I grabbed the creature by the neck,

"Take me to where this Titus lives."

I eased my grip

and let the creature slip

down to the dirt,

where it slithered off toward the Fringe.

The Fringe was home to the City's worst,

soul traders and meat marketeers,

a pitiless black hole

where there was no friend, no foe,

only deals to be struck

for what one held most dear.

It was worse than I thought.

When we arrived there were things

I couldn't describe,

and now, once seen, I couldn't deny,

inhuman delights, all for the right price,

along with the madness it brings.

The creature tried to take flight

as we entered the man-child's tent.

The healer was just about

to install my heart in a doll

made of mud and odd bits

when I offered a trade instead.

"My heart for this piece of flesh,"

I held the creature by the scruff.

Titus Healing eyed me quick,

he licked his lips

and handed me my heart,

which still beat for my long-lost love.

He grabbed the creature and tore it apart,
I didn't wait to see the rest.
I found a quiet spot
and once alone, I pulled the poultice out
and gently placed my tattered heart
back into the cavern of my chest.

I could feel it sputter, then restart,
a beat that quickened my resolve
to pay my penance
and awake from this sentence,
and find my way back
to that memory where it all went wrong.

The Great and the Small

In the Underland
one has nothing but time
to ponder, or wander
if one is so inclined,
and think about the misdeeds
and misappropriations
and miscreant behaviors
that cleaved the air
and brought one here
to dwell among
the murderers and thieves.
It soon becomes apparent,
there are no small creatures
crawling upon this pitiless floor.
No spiders, no mice,
not even a nest of snakes
to make this hideous existence
all the more hideous
a torture to endure.

No, one soon realizes

that man is the only creature

of higher learning,

the only creature that takes

this blessing and turns it

into something dirty,

forsakes the godly gift

of learning by one's mistakes

and perverts its only intention

into avarice and greed.

Of all creatures great and small,

man can be the least

to understand the limitless

potential given freely to thee.

The Chair of Absolution

The Chair of Absolution was not
just a piece of furniture but a man,
a man who chose to council the most
inconsolable souls who inhabited the Underland.

His disfigurements were legend,
a unique condition that had no name,
when he absolved you your indiscretions,
a portion was absorbed into his bent and buckled frame.

His office was a crumbling grotto
whose walls were wet with luminescent streams,
appointments were only for those
who wandered close in the throes of a waking dream.

It was there I found myself
roused by two assistants to the Chair,
"Your dream has brought you here," it grumbled,
"but you must take the final step. Are you prepared?"

The Chair was both man and stone,
a large squarish seat carved into the wall.
It was difficult to tell where flesh ended and chair began,
"Come sit," it said, and my feet obeyed as if hearing a distant call.

And when I sat, I felt absorbed,
as my body sank into its flesh,
"I can't take it all," it whispered,
"but I can take some, it's up to you to absolve the rest."

And for the first time my conscience recalled
a name from my past inglorious life,
her name was Emily and she had golden hair
and emerald eyes and she was my wedded wife.

I cheated on her with several women
even though my love for her I did profess,
we even talked of having children, but between my work
and late-night affairs we saw each other less and less.

What I remembered next struck me cold,
colder than the coldest day in the world above,
I recalled the evening I arrived home with flowers
and found her—my dear sweet Emily—in a bath of her own blood.

I tore myself free from the Chair of Absolution,
leaving bits and pieces of myself behind,
and staggered from the grotto shaken,
memories of Emily playing over and over in my mind.

The Mimic

For days, I wandered the city a broken man,
more broken than that first day in the catacombs.
I cursed the Underland and its lack of death
when it would be a mercy instead of an eternity tortured and alone.

What perverted God would create such a prison?
I would have cursed its name if I had known.
At last, I stopped, collapsing against one
of the myriad hovels, sobbing, shaking, chilled down to the bone.

It was then I heard the singing,
a warbling melody of startling beauty unrefined.
Could it be? My Emily? It was the song she used sing
while gardening. Or had I completely lost my mind?

When I peered inside the hovel,
there was no one there that I could see, then something stirred,
a hideous deformity rose up into the weak candlelight,
a creature so ugly and yet could sing as beautifully as a bird.

53

"As a bird... as a bird," it said, it read my thoughts
and spoke a perfect imitation of my voice.
A mimic. I'd heard rumors of such creatures,
so ancient, so depraved they are a living witness to the void.

What the Chair of Absolution gave, perhaps
the mimic could provide the rest, I thought,
and so I asked: "Emily... Am I responsible for her death?
And, if so, how can I ever recover what I've lost?"

"She is here... she is here... like a bird... she is here,"
the mimic sang, this time in Emily's voice so sweet.
All the time I'd wasted searching within
when there was only one place where she could be.

"How do I get there?" I asked the mimic,

and it shambled close in all its putrid decay,

and whispered with breath tainted with death,

"The Idol...the Idol...find the Idol...it knows the way."

I left the mimic to its singing,

remembering what the Chair of Absolution had said,

the Chair took from me what was needed to lift the scales

from my memory, and now it was up to me to perform the rest.

And so I set out in that moment to find

the Idol of the Uncommitted, committed in my quest.

My dear sweet Emily, I'm coming for thee,

to resurrect our love beyond eternity, beyond even death.

Where the Sun Shines Never

In the world above

we are taught to love

and cherish all life that exists,

because once it's gone

it's gone forever.

But here in this world I live,

a place where the sun shines never,

where death is dead

and life a perpetual punishment,

I've come to understand

why those in the Underland

huddle in hovels and squatters' pits

in eternal penance resigned.

Because redemption grows

in small increments,

there is no model to follow,

no pattern well-defined,

the path is obscured,

the task immense,

we are on our own and yet

the signs I've seen,

the words I've heard

tell me I'm very much alive.

I must remind myself

of these very things,

every minute of every hour

of every day without the sun,

that this betterment

toward which I endeavor,

this dream I walk through nightly

like a ghost in search of flesh,

is all the reason I need

to believe it can be done.

The Twin Cities

The women, it was whispered,

communed and congregated in a distant place,

another dark and dirty city without a proper name,

set apart like college dorms

on some immense subterranean plane.

Imagine the chaos, the debauchery, that would ensue,

all that macho bravado that swells the head,

that our quest for sex makes us do,

it was not surprising this realm was designed

to separate the two.

But truth be told, something as impermanent

as sexual gratification was farthest from my thoughts,

my heart still beat for another in that life I tore apart,

a love I didn't know was love

until the light of hope was all but lost.

For she is the reason I subsist on dreams and dreams alone.

I believed, if I must spend an eternity here

drowning in a sea of agony till I atone,

I will if it means one day

I will find my way back home.

But sometimes it felt I lived in two cities,

one of moral desperation and one of solitary need,

one path leading toward salvation, the other toward disease,

one half of my heart a soft and pliable thing,

the other half deadened by defeat.

So I went to the Idol of the Uncommitted and kneeled,

my body twisted, my skin a painful patchwork

of open sores that would not heal,

and asked forgiveness with the good half of my heart

and hoped the truth would be revealed.

I heard a grinding sound, and around I turned,

and although alone I was in the presence of something new:

a section of stones in the city wall had moved.

A doorway? An answer? I thought.

Or just an entrance to another ancient tomb?

In that moment, so many doubts went through my head,

should I follow this path into the wall

or return to the miserable life I'd eked out here instead?

I approached the opening and stepped inside,

the wall sealed tight and darkness tumbled in.

Inside the Walls of the City that Never Sleeps

There are realities and there are truths,
and there are things in between,
worlds within worlds in the folds of the Earth
with a myriad of pathways unseen.
Such was the case inside the walls
of the City That Never Sleeps.

The darkness diffused to a yellowish glow,
lighting the passageway's twists and turns.
Strange fungi crawled on both ceiling and wall
like the veins of a giant worm.
In which direction I strode or what toward
was impossible to discern.

I possessed no map, no compass dial,
that could have assisted in my quest,
only an innate trust and a faith in my gut
that this passage would grant success,
that it would lead me to the threshold
of my love and nothing less.

Through spaces too narrow, too jagged,
too deadly for a weaker man, I crawled,
swimming over the bones no doubt left by those
who had unceremoniously risked it all.
Perhaps this was the death I sought,
I thought, inside the city's walls.

As I trekked, my deformities began
to recede like the veil of a dream,
my pace grew strong as I hurried along
reinvigorated by what it might mean:
I was close and getting closer
to the one thing that meant the world to me.

In the between, neither inside nor out,
like a wormhole carved through time,
the passageway led me to a place
that was unreachable from outside,
a secret doorway in the stone
like the one I'd left behind.

I emerged, bloodied and bruised,
expecting to see a sister realm,
a sprawling vista all too familiar,
the differences too difficult to tell,
a twin city of mercurial clouds
and choking sulfurous smells.

I stood instead a spectator
in an antiseptic room,
a metronomic beat of machinery
replaced the Underland's mournful gloom,
ahead lay a patient in a hospital bed
fed by a myriad of tubes.

A woman stood in solemn silence
beside the comatose man,
her expression unmoved, her stance resolute,
a clutch of documents in her hand.
"Emily?" I said, "is that you?"
my mind grappling to understand.

Elated and confused I moved
across the intervening space,
to be by Emily's side, to prove I was alive,
that our love had found its way,
she wore dark glasses but I could see
the bruises still on her face.

Bruises from my hand, I recalled,
in a drunken stupor before I left,
an angry man with violent hands
and selfish heart and soul bereft,
that night I was beaten in an alley,
robbed and left for dead.

Emily didn't shed a tear
as she signed the papers in her hand,
a legal right to end my life
heroic measures be damned.
Did I blame her? No. And so
I returned to the Underland.

Back I stepped, back through stone
that was but a figment of my mind,
I retraced my path and as time passed
my cancerous tumors multiplied,
I could barely crawl as the wall opened up
on the city I'd left behind.

More hideous than any denizen,
unrecognizable as once a man,
I dragged and scraped my twisted frame
back to what I now understand,
back to where I belonged all along
at home in the Underland.

OTHER MACABRE MACHINATIONS

The Underwater Circus

"Come down by the lakeside,"

called the circus clown with his sad faced makeup on.

The curious were drawn as nighttime fell,

like moths to the colored lights, the carousel.

My brother tagged along as I was drawn as well.

We saw the lights, we heard the music, and something else.

A sound found only on the radio,

in between stations where the static pools and the emptiness dwells.

And still, we followed like all the rest,

past the sad faced clown to the water's edge.

And there beneath the surface,

swam the multicolored shimmer of the underwater circus.

There was no price of admission,

just the light of our souls to keep the rides spinning.

I watched in horror as each by each,

the town's people sank to the bottom to the circus beneath.

But when I felt the cold water

creep over my skin, I turned to my brother.

"Grab some mud and plug your ears

and run, there's something evil happening here!"

Now, evil is a strong word and I was still young,

what's evil to others can be beautiful to some.

I'd like to say I saved both my brother

and I that day, but only one of us escaped the water.

And it was as beautiful as advertised,

the sounds in my ears, the lights in my eyes.

There were circus animals with cotton candy wings,

swimming circles above the crowds and everything.

There was music all around as if in a dream,

and laughter so loud it could be mistaken for screams.

I knew my brother and I were not the same,

I was more spirited while he played it safe.

So, I sank to the bottom to join the rest,

on the long carousel ride of death.

And I've been here, now, for fifty years this way,

each year a different town, a different lake.

So, if you see a clown one day

calling, "Come down by the lakeside"—run away!

But if you have no fear of what lies beneath the surface,

come join us here at the underwater circus.

The Cottage on the Lake

The rental agent smiled as I signed my name on the winter lease,
I then gave her a check for security deposit plus first and last month's rent.
She nervously shook my hand and promptly handed me the keys,
"Good luck," she said, then hurried out the door, got into her car and left.

I didn't understand how a lakeside cottage so beautiful could be so cheap,
fully furnished, kitchen appliances, utilities included in the monthly check.
I moved my belongings in that weekend, and on the first night,
        before I went to sleep,
I spent the last hour of the evening in a chair alone upon the deck.

The night air blew fresh and warm across the surface of the lake,
the lap of the water, the creak of the dock, such peaceful sounds to my ear.
But when I heard the whisper I, at first, believed it was a neighbor
        staying up late,
but the adjacent cottages were dark and unoccupied this time of year.

I thought nothing of it and went to bed, exhausted from the move,
but that night I dreamed of a woman in a sleeping gown standing on the dock.
She stared out across the open water under the light of a pregnant moon.
I rushed to prevent her from jumping in, but before I could I heard the clock.

70

My morning alarm woke me up to another brilliant autumn day,
another pleasant realization that was just too hard to believe.
I was once again on my own and in a beautiful cottage on the lake,
where I could spend my hours alone with no pressures placed on me.

But when nighttime fell and surrounded the cottage with its dark,
I found myself looking out the window for reasons I could not explain.
Once again, before going to bed, I sat outside beneath the stars,
and watched the moonlight slither like a serpent across the lake.

This time, I was awakened from my resting spot atop the deck,
by the sobbing of a young woman who stood on the wooden dock below.
I got up and slowly approached her, the breeze a soft caress.
"Hello?" I said. She turned and, though startled, made no move to go.

She had long dark hair and eyes as sad as flowers in the rain,
and she wore only a sleeping gown with no shoes upon her feet.
I invited her to leave the water and come inside my cottage on the lake,
but she smiled the saddest smile and then threw herself into the deep.

I awoke then, my hands still gripping tight the deck chair arms,
my heart pounding like a hammer nailing spikes into my chest.
She was gone, this woman, this apparition, this love reflection, she was gone,
and I was never, ever going to get her back again.

The days and months that followed were a silent wintery chill,
spent in the company of myself both in dream and wide awake.
I have to say I loved the one who came to visit and always will,
the one who lies beneath the water at the cottage on the lake.

Phantastikon

This doppelganger
from time past
that appears to me,
that mirrors me.

This interloper—
distant, fleeting,
yet near enough for
fear to reach.

This phantastikon—
this reverie;
this inner spell toward
which I'm drawn.

This apparition—
this ghostly witness
that speaks of visions
from beyond.

The Fetch

She appears as wisp and vapor,
wearing a gown of diaphanous thread.
She is you and yet not you,
at least, she is not you yet.

She follows your every movement,
to the market; when you brush your teeth.
She is a shadow with your likeness,
a reflection no one can see.

You should be frightened of her presence,
but you feel a kinship in her gaze.
She doesn't speak, but if she did,
you know what she would say.

She would say I am here for you—
you and your tired, heavy soul.
Come to me when you are ready
and together we'll be whole.

One day you stop ignoring her
and confront her where she stands.
You detect a smile that might be your own
as she quietly takes your hand.

The Malingering

He was slumped against the sidewalk wall,

just another homeless creature passed out from too much waste.

You gave a wide berth as you entered your gated living quarters,

but you couldn't avoid the smell.

The odor was more age and decay than filth,

a miasma of malignant dreams and malcontent.

It clung like cigarette smoke clings to a damp jacket,

although no one could smell it but you.

"What's the matter, sweetheart?" your wife asks,

as she greets you at the door with a kiss.

Your daughter shrieks "Daddy!" as she runs with open arms.

You kiss your wife and hug your daughter as if there's nothing wrong.

You shrug it off without a mention,

but the smell is just too cloying to deny.

With it comes a feeling of utter despair

that grows stronger as nighttime comes.

Your dreams are wrought with violent images,

and you wake up with the sheets damp around you.

You go to the window and look toward the streetlamp

and see a portion of the man who still lies there.

So you don an overcoat with something heavy in its pocket,

uncode the front door alarm and quietly slip out.

You walk down to the gate and step onto the sidewalk

and confront the homeless man.

"You have to leave," you ask him politely,

as your hand grips the trunk of a brass elephant bookend.

Somehow you know who this derelict is and why he is there.

You also know there can be only one of you.

The collection of torn garments stirs then straightens,

and a pair of fathomless eyes bore into your soul.

His voice is deep and the ground shakes with its timbre,

"I'm afraid, my friend," he says, "it is you who has to leave."

75

What happens then is difficult to recall,

as your hand comes down with two blows to the head

with a force and fury you didn't think you were capable,

and a guttural scream from a place unknown.

The next thing you remember is you're back in your bed

surrounded by the comfort and safety of your wife and home.

It's morning and your daughter runs in and jumps onto the covers,

"Wake up," she says, "I'm hungry!"

You're thankful because you can no longer smell that smell,

that death knell odor of dreams gone by.

"What's wrong?" you ask your wife as she wrinkles her nose.

Your daughter laughs and says, "Pew... Daddy farted."

You sniff yourself but there's nothing to detect,

but you rush to the shower just the same.

That strange dream you had that has you wrapped in a fog—

you're hoping you can cleanse it away.

But one look in the mirror tells you nothing will ever be normal again,

as a pair of fathomless eyes bore into your soul.

You feel the weight of your decisions like a damp overcoat.

A guttural scream soon follows.

The Soul that Knew No Solace

Those cursed chains of grief that bound me,
That kept me prisoner of unspeakable things
    I wished had never found me,
But I devised a way to escape those painful memories
     that circled around me:
I gave up my very soul.

And once my soul was forever forsaken,
My nightly excesses became uncontrolled,
     now served by a conscience that would never awaken.
It's cold, I know, but I traveled the road
     many have dreamed but few have taken;
But, for this, there was a price.

And the price was for every unholy behavior,
A piece of my body would wither and die,
     revealing the depths of my true nature,
A finger, an ear, a patch of hair, an eye—
     in the mirror I became a hideous stranger;
I didn't know how but it had to stop.

So I searched for the soul I had so callously abandoned;
I found it in the eyes and smile of my three-year-old niece
        in whom innocence still lay pure and undamaged.
I prayed that the Gods would accept the sacrifice of one so sweet
        in return for the one thing I demanded,
And returned my soul they did.

Now here I am whole again,
But these chains of grief still bind me
        down deep in my soul again,
And keep me prisoner of unspeakable things,
        irredeemable things that are sure to take their toll again.
Her face will haunt me to my grave.

Funeral for Annette

I was dreaming a seemingly harmless dream, when
I was awakened by two women I'd hardly met.
"Today's the day," they said,
"It's time to pay your respects."
They took me then
to attend the funeral for Annette.

They took me half-naked against my will,
down a subterranean corridor long and wet.
"Where are you taking me!"
I pressed, repeating until
their eyes took aim,
"It's time to pay your respects."

We surfaced under a sky pregnant with stars,
in the woods that rimmed the campus, I could only guess.
I tried to remember in which direction
we had traveled and how far.
Not thinking instead
Who was Annette? And why was she dead?

Beyond the woods there stood a graveyard wall,
they dragged me to a place where the graves were still fresh.
They pushed me to the ground,
and there I crawled.
On a headstone, I read
the name engraved: Annette.

Annie? my memory recalled as thick as the mist
that covered the ground against my chest.
"We met at a party, okay?
We danced and we kissed..."
I felt a heel on my neck
and together they said: "What happened next?"

"Nothing! I saw something—someone—better and bailed.
Annie was perfectly fine when I left!"
But that wasn't true was it? I thought
as the memory became more detailed.
When I saw Annie next,
her makeup had run and her eyes were red.

"She was our sister, our bright shining sister,"
said the woman with her foot on my neck.
I heard a shovel hit the dirt,
"We will forever miss her."
The digging began then
right alongside the grave for Annette.

My mind raced... What could I say
that would bring this nightmare to an end?
As the hole grew deeper
at a frightening pace,
I realized then
only one thing could be said.

"I'm sorry," I cried, and the digging ceased,
and the pressure released from my neck.
"That's all we wanted.
Annette would be pleased.
You paid your respects,
now you are free of your debt."

Free? We come into this world with nothing
and leave full of guilt and regret.
I rose from the ground,
grabbed the shovel and suddenly
swung right and swung left
and struck both sisters dead.

"I'm sorry," I lied, and slid them into the hole
beside the headstone for their sister Annette,
and I covered their bodies with the dirt
they had planned for my soul.
Stained with blood and with sweat,
I returned to my dorm room to rest.

When I woke the next morning I was not alone,
there was a beautiful young woman in my bed.
"Good morning," she whispered,
but it was somber in tone,
and I knew then
today was the funeral for Annette.

Bone Riders

We cling wetly to
this multi-jointed frame,
riding all day long
through howling wind
and pelting rain,
through sun-filled warmth
beneath clear blue skies,
we ride,
until the damp earth burns
to desert sand,
and daylight turns
to eternal night,
and we leave at last
these bones behind
for a different kind
of journey.

The Promise of Eternity

A body, a tree,

carved with runic symbols,

letters cut to indignify

a heinous crime with mystery.

The man, a priest,

black robe rustling in the wind,

crows perched on gnarled branches

voicing their objection to the interruption of their feast.

With bible gripped in rigor mortised hand,

the holy man was taken down,

arcane symbols jutting from his brow

in a hideous bas relief.

The tree, a sprawling oak,

used for Sunday family picnics

or a meeting place for lovers under moonlit gaze,

possessed a darker, much more sinister history.

A hanging tree, in less enlightened days,

when man presumed command of evil

and yet evil had the upper hand,

when poor folk and knotted rope were on display for all to see.

A familiar landmark, a respected figure,

both connected by this unholy act of desecration,

perpetrated by a person or persons rooted

in the rolling landscape of the surrounding community.

But the Inspector Chief and his deputy

determined cause of death a suicide,

the ancient symbols self-inflicted, a troubled man,

a lonely life, guilty of some unforgivable personal atrocity.

At the funeral, the line of parishioners
snaked outside the gates of the cemetery,
stunned at the event that has left them wondering
does God still hear their prayers or is this the death of divinity?

The crows now roost in what has
once again become the hanging tree,
above the head stones where beneath,
it is said, all God's creatures rest in peace.

While the Inspector Chief and his followers
meet beneath the new moon of a vacant night
to worship the darkness they have brought into their midst,
in exchange for gifts and the promise of eternity.

The Crows of Las Cruces

The crows of Las Cruces
descended in flocks
of thousands or more,
settling blackly, thickly
upon the rocks,
and dry dust desert floor.

At first no thought
was given twice,
for stranger things have flown
in on the desert wind
to stay the night
and rest their bones.

> "They're here to raise the dead,"
> the old Native woman said,
> sitting at her roadside stand,
> painting crows on smooth round stones
> with blinded-eye and crippled-hand.

With summer past
the nights grew long,
each one blacker than before.
The townspeople waited
for the crows to move on,
but in flew several thousand more.

And though they flooded
the streets in town
and perched in curtains on the eaves,
it was the cemetery where
they eventually touched down,
the place, it is said, where no one leaves.

> "They're here to make the dead alive,"
> the old Native woman cried,
> sitting at her roadside stand,
> weaving strings into bird-like things
> with blinded-eye and crippled-hand.

But no one paid
the old woman heed,
for the dead had never slipped
out from beneath
the desert scrub and weed
or breached a family crypt.

And so it was
on All Hallows' Eve,
the crows began to stretch their wings.
While children, dressed
in make believe,
collected candy-coated things.

     "The dead are coming home,"
     the old Native woman was heard to groan,
     before closing up her roadside stand,
     a talisman for each child's grin
     with curious-eye and outstretched-hand.

One by one, into
the starlit night,
to the edge of town the children were led
their spirits strong,
their energy bright,
to the cemetery to jumpstart the dead.

But as the children descended
upon the graveyard stones,
the crows of Las Cruces had fled.
In their place were the old
Native woman's bones
and a note in the sand that read:

> "Go home, young ones, to sleep,
> I have given the dead my soul to keep.
> But the gifts I gave to you will bind.
> Remember me on All Hallows' Eve,
> for when your breath leaves, your soul is mine."

The Crows of Las Cruces Revisited

Now fifty years
have come and gone,
the children flown
to every corner of
the country and beyond
to lead lives of their own.

But in their dreams
they often hear,
as if without a choice,
a plaintive whisper
in their ear
of an old Native woman's voice.

> "Your time is setting like the sun.
> Your soul is mine, my little one."
> And in each dream a crow appears
> with beady eye as black as night
> to wake them in a grip of fear.

The talismans sat
on tables and shelves,
a keepsake they couldn't lose.
The children, now grown,
had forgotten the spell
that bound them in their youth.

But one by one,
as their death drew near,
Las Cruces came to mind.
A vacation in the town
they once held so dear,
but had chosen to leave behind.

> "The older the crow, the weaker the breath,
> the softer the heart, the sweeter the death,"
> the old Native woman cawed in their sleep,
> as they flew into town from all around
> to at last find a sense of peace.

But peace was fleeting
as All Hallows' Eve loomed
and the town prepared.
Each brought their talisman
back home to roost,
some packed it unaware.

They met at the Las Cruces Inn
on the thirty-first,
each dressed in black,
and conspired to undo
the old Native woman's curse
and leave their souls intact.

> "From beyond the grave, I'll be reborn
> when the moonlight fades into the morn,"
> the old Native woman groaned
> throughout the day inside the brains
> of those who had been called back home.

As the Las Cruces streets
filled with kids
running from door to door,
some stopped for treats
at the Las Cruces Inn
and received something more.

Smooth round stones
with painted crows
were placed in buckets and bags,
the unsuspecting children
would go home
not knowing what they had.

And so on All Hallows' Day it came to light,
a group of elderly travelers died during the night
at the Las Cruces Inn where each of them stayed.
Each was found hands clasped, peaceful at last,
with what looked like a smile upon their face.

The Black Star Traveling Show

When The Black Star Traveling Show comes to town,
dead birds dot the trail behind like breadcrumbs,
and flowers wither in their beds and fill the air
with their rancid fragrance.

When The Black Star Traveling Show comes to town,
men who never raised their hand against their wives
leave purple blossoms upon their loved ones' faces
and the seeds of hatred planted in their hearts.

When The Black Star Traveling Show comes to town,
it brings a cold, bone-chilling wind from the pit of space
that turns the sunlit skies grey with clouds
that hang low like a crushing anvil.

When The Black Star Traveling Show comes to town,
the night becomes a long and restless place
where the silent screams of fading dreams
join the creeping call of chaos.

Dancing in the Dark

It seemed like such harmless fun,
You weren't hurting anyone,
Dancing with a fervor
Only a heart inclined toward murder can do.
Just remember, when dancing in the dark,
The dark dances with you.

To pass the time, you dipped and spun,
You weren't hurting anyone,
Dancing with precision
On a crowded floor with victim number two.
Just remember, when dancing in the dark,
The dark dances with you.

They didn't turn, they didn't run,
You weren't hurting anyone,
Dancing with a satisfaction
That only comes after the passion is through.
Just remember, when dancing in the dark,
The dark dances with you.

Night after night, till the rise of the sun,

You weren't hurting anyone,

Dancing with a vengeance,

All the while ignoring the elephant in the room.

Just remember, when dancing in the dark,

The dark dances with you.

The contest has only just begun,

You weren't hurting anyone,

Dancing with the horror

There has only ever been one partner for you, it's true.

Just remember, when dancing in the dark,

The dark dances with you.

The Suckling

That sound! That sound!

It follows me like a slave duty-bound.

Oh, how I long for the days of quiet peace I once found.

That sound... that sound...

That mewling, drooling suckling sound.

It was joy, a selfish joy,

that filled my heart, I must admit,

that steered my lovesick mind toward the crimes I'd soon commit,

the joy of just the two of us

hand-in-hand, romantic dinners candle-lit.

I was a happy man,

more happy than no man deserved to be,

with an attentive wife, an affectionate wife—

my dear sweet Emily.

From the very start, she gave heart unconditionally.

We wed, oh, yes we wed

on a beautiful sunlit day in June.

Then we traveled to the mountains for our honeymoon.

It was a blissful week

of nights beneath the sheets and sleeping till the hour of noon.

But with such intensity

came the immensity of responsibility that followed.

When Emily told me she was pregnant, I could barely swallow.

The news left me reeling,

numb to feeling as if I were headed for the gallows.

So, I devised a plan

to rid this interloper from my dear sweet Emily,

a remedy, a tea, to nip the bud of this accidental seed.

But I made the cure too strong

and killed the one thing that meant everything to me.

And nearly nine months to the day

Emily and I had spent that weekend in the clouds,

I awoke in the middle of the night to a sickening suckling sound.

It was the child I didn't want

come back to haunt me for the heinous act I carried out.

It cried, it gurgled,

it wailed a wet, unassailable song.

It carried on like an underwater banshee from dusk till dawn.

No sooner would I turn off the light

and fall sleep, my quiet peace would soon be gone.

Of course my eyes

could not confirm the assault upon my ears.

The second I would flick the lamp switch, the sounds would disappear

and an empty bedroom,

devoid of tiny monsters, would greet my mounting fear.

The only evidence I had

that a physical event had taken place,

was a wet spot along the bed sheet's edge in close proximity to my face.

So close, in fact,

I should have felt the breath of the thing that left its trace.

It was then I grew afraid

my mind was playing tricks of the most devious kind.

A guilt-ridden conscience carrying a secret too great to hide.

That the mouth the suckling sound

had made was indeed mine and only mine.

The weeks and months

that followed have been torturous at best,

most times I lay in a fetal position upon my empty bed,

mewling like some

wounded offspring kicked from the proverbial nest.

Emily, dear sweet Emily,

oh, how I wish your life had not been taken.

I feel my mind has descended into a somnambulant sea of lactation,

a sleepless eternity drenched

in a nightmare from which I cannot awaken.

And now I think it's time

I seek the quiet peace that I once found.

To allow myself the dignity of a quick release before I slowly drown

in that sound... that sound...

that unholy, mewling, drooling suckling sound.

Redcap

Redcap creeps along
late night country roads,
searching for that yellow glow,
the broken sleep of restless souls
awake when all the rest
have surrendered to the land of dreams.

Redcap breathes in heavy gasps,
halts and heaves,
his insides dying,
the red cap drying in the wind,
the need to whet his red cap's appetite
for blood a cruel necessity.

And so, at last, he stops to gaze,
outside a lonely farmhouse
kitchen window frame,
the tinkling of a teacup
signaling an after midnight
date with destiny.

Whispers Beyond the Glass

I

Mr. Adams should have drawn the window blinds
when the first fat flakes began to fly.
His classroom was just too restless knowing
when they arrived home after school it would still be snowing.

For days it fell, a cold and smothering frozen ghost.
Miskatonic Falls Elementary had never
closed its doors due to inclement weather.
But Mr. Adams lived within walking distance, as did most.

Children, bundled layer upon layer, trudged their way
to school each morning as they played.
Teachers, who knew a good education mattered,
dutifully taught their subjects while the snowfall gathered.

But Mr. Adams' class began to dwindle one by one.
He couldn't help but feel the isolation creeping,
as the snow's depth kept increasing.
He wished for it to end but had an inkling it had only just begun.

II

Miskatonic Falls had all but disappeared
beneath the worst snowfall in years.
With power gone the residents stoked their fireplaces.
Life continued on, help would come, and so they waited.

Mr. Adams taught his class amid the hiss of propane gas,
and though the blinds were drawn against what was yonder,
the children's eyes still did wander
as if listening to voices whispered through the glass.

The students continued to disappear day by day,
the empty chairs matched the stares of those who still remained.
Abandoned, orphaned, neglected, forgotten—
what else had this unending storm brought them?

For Mr. Adams, the answers were not written on any board.
Not only were there whispers outside the casements,
there came strange and strangled cries up from the basement,
cries that could no longer be ignored.

III

Miskatonic Falls Elementary had fallen still,
no faculty, no children had braved the winter chill.
All except Mr. Adams, his flashlight beam crawling
down the basement stairs toward the voices he heard calling.

For three weeks now the snow had emptied from the sky,
against each door a gentle rapping,
unrelenting in its window tapping,
as if determined to fill the void inside.

Mr. Adams had known such emptiness from the start,
with no family, no wife, no children to fill his heart.
He entered the now cold boiler room, the voices willing
him deeper into the crawl spaces of the building.

At last, he came upon an opening cold and bright,
like an entrance to another world slowly turning.
As the voices spoke of those deserving,
offering the answer to his yearning, he stepped into the light.

Beyond the Blue Veil

On our maiden voyage across the sea,

we witnessed a strange blue apparition where none should be,

a curtain of rain, we thought, or wall of mist,

    of a color both rich and pale

that a crew member named the blue veil.

But as we approached, our curiosity piqued,

the air turned cold and clouds formed dark and bleak.

A storm took hold and tossed us like a barnacle

    on the back of an angry whale,

and we lost sight of the blue veil.

The crew held on day and night with little sleep,

fighting wind and rain and mammoth waves with white foam peaks.

Just when it appeared our names would become part

    of some sad sea-faring tale,

we reached the calm beyond the blue veil.

Such ominous beauty yawned before us as we stood upon the deck,
a verdant land as lush and long as any fertile coastal neck
sat upon the ocean calm as if gifted by the Gods for our travails,
for having gone beyond the blue veil.

But God's gifts can sometimes be not what one expects.
When half the crew boarded a skiff and rowed to shore,
  they were promptly met
by a naked tribe of hominids waving frantically
  as if to warn us to turn back and set our sails,
to take us back before we tacked beyond the blue veil.

The instant our crew set foot upon the beach's head,
they began to grunt and drool, their arms hung low,
  their statures bent,
like the native hominids they too waved their arms
  and beseeched us with their primitive wails
for us to leave this strange lagoon for the blue veil.

With half our crew now lost to some unknown regressive trait,
we raised sail and caught a breeze that took us from the reef
      into the ocean waves,
back to the very spot where we fought for our lives against
      the pelting rain and blowing gales,
back to, back through, the waiting aqua haze of the blue veil.

Back forward into time we swept, from blue into the grey,
back into the blackened storm that, before, had nearly
      sent us to our graves,
our skeleton crew performed as admirably as any the sea
      had ever seen set sail,
as we mourned our loss and moved beyond the blue veil.

Now many a nautical mile separate us from the incident of that day,
but a distressing and most vile condition has gripped
      the men that still remain,
their sudden brutish behavior has me exiled in my cabin,
      with physical changes on every scale,
cursing all the while the day we voyaged beyond the blue veil.

The Memory of Persistence

Above the earth and sea,

in galaxies too numerous to behold,

on planets spun by strange gravities

both bountiful and stark,

in forests thick and green

and in rivers deep and cold,

there exists a memory as ancient

as the first star to brave the dark.

A memory that can be found

in every dreamer ever told,

a memory in every stone

in every glacier on the march,

a memory of origin

as powerful as it is old,

a memory that keeps the universe

from tearing itself apart.

Beyond the farthest horizon,

in space that bends and folds,

on distant shores that crash

on sands that glitter and spark,

in all things great and small

it is written in their code,

a memory that will now

and forever leave its mark.

The Illustrations of Robert Ingram Price

Jeffrey Thomas was eating tuna from a tin
when the stories arrived by post,
a bit of illustration work sent by a publisher friend,
a gift—a handout seen by most.

But Jeffrey's dignity was hard to bruise,
he was once as good as the rest,
before women and liquor fed his life to the blues
and the deadlines came and went unmet.

Illustrating these stories was his second chance
(more like his third or fourth, truth be told),
so he went to the attic to find his pens
and found they were too worn and too old.

Without money for replacements, he'd have to make do,
so he sat down and read the manuscript twice:
stories both realistically horrific and true
by the author Robert Ingram Price.

Price's life was as short-lived and fantastic as his words,
he'd been a practitioner of the occult,
until he disappeared, never again seen or heard,
until the discovery of these stories in a vault.

So, Jeffrey began, as sober as sin,
drunk on Price's inspiration,
sketching and stippling away with his pens,
surprised at the quality of the illustrations.

It was as if his pens had returned anew,
as sharp and as crisp as before.
For Jeffrey, the question wasn't how such things could be true,
but rather, in this case, how long could it be ignored?

Panel after panel came to life beneath his hand,
one horrific image after the next,
creatures of the night both of the sky and the land,
as if birthed from the stories' text.

Until, at last, the illustrations were complete,

Jeffrey's pens now as fresh as the day they were bought.

From out of the shadows there came the shuffling of feet,

and Jeffrey turned to see what his efforts had wrought.

A curious little man, a hundred years lost,

stood there with a dark glint in his eye.

"Thank you, my friend," he spoke, then he paused,

before slipping through the wall out of sight.

Jeffrey Thomas had indeed been given a second chance,

and his pens stayed forever brilliant and bright.

His illustrations are now featured on every magazine stand,

thanks to the helping hand of Robert Ingram Price.

Outside These Chamber Walls

Why, why do I waste my time
on every thought, on every rhyme,
when there is so much more to see
outside these chamber walls?

My mind, my mind is full of words,
circling, circling like carrion birds,
waiting for each thought to die
upon the fallow page.

For once, for once I'd like to be
a man whose heart beats naturally,
who speaks the truth without revision,
consequences be damned.

But no, hell no, I hesitate,
unsure which words to orchestrate
the perfect thought, the perfect lie,
while the world spins on without me.

This curse, this curse I must profess
is but a penance, nothing less,
for every sentence left unsaid
to those whom I once loved.

And so, I write, I write, I write,
to find the words once trapped inside,
so that, one day, I may leave this room,
my conscience unburdened.

A Pen and a Promise to Keep

Edgar, dear Edgar, you have unfairly
Drawn the task too tall to meet,
Giving us such dark visions it barely
Allows my pen one sentence complete.
Rest assured I will not tire, however,

Attempt as I might, I know I will never
Leave as great a mark as you have done,
Let me at least achieve a smaller one?
Allow me this and I will offer my soul,
Nevermore will your tales be unheard.

Poetry will rise and I'll act out the role,
Only you will provide every word.
Edgar, dear Edgar, I give you my word.

His Horror's Masterful Voice

Ever since poor Edgar caught his deathly chill,
Drunken debate has raged and likely always will.
Greatest of all horror writers of this earthly realm?
All must consider Poe nearest the helm.
Ravens had never achieved such notoriety before.

As well, a severed heart still beating 'neath a floor.
Let us not forget Hopfrog's gruesome table turn.
Likewise the fate of Fortunato should forever earn
A place for Poe atop the legions who have tried.
None have tapped so easily into the fear inside.

Perhaps I should restrain what I'm about to confess here,
Occasionally I hear Poe's voice whispering in my ear.
Excuse me, but I believe the end is near.

ACKNOWLEDGEMENTS

Songs of the Underland

originally appeared in *Cosmic Horror Monthly*, 2021

"The Underland,"

"The Balance of the World,"

"The Song of the Underland,"

"The Mercurial Clouds of Misery,"

originally appeared in *Spectral Realms*, 2022

"As the Dream Descends"

Other Macabre Machinations

originally appeared in *Life Among the Dream Merchants*, 2005

"The Crows of Las Cruces"

originally appeared in _The Book of Night_, 2015

"The Black Star Traveling Show,"

"Phantastikon,"

"The Soul That Knew No Solace,"

"Beyond the Blue Veil,"

"The Illustrations of Robert Ingram Price,"

"The Crows of Las Cruces Revisited,"

"The Cottage on the Lake"

"A Pen and a Promise to Keep"

originally appeared in _Darkling's Beasts and Brews_, 2017

"Redcap"

originally appeared in _Spectral Realms_, 2018

"Bone Riders"

"A Promise of Eternity"

originally appeared in _Spectral Realms_, 2019

"The Underwater Circus"

originally appeared in _Macabre Museum_, 2019

"The Malingering"

originally appeared in _Eye to the Telescope_, 2019

"The Fetch"

Afterword

The Rhyme of the Ancient Rock Star

This is my second full-length collection of (mostly) rhyming poetry. My first, Life Among the Dream Merchants, was published seventeen years ago and was a tribute to both H.P. Lovecraft and Edgar Allan Poe. You might think you'll have to wait another seventeen years for another collection, but that urge to rhyme has always been with me and, I suspect, always will.

In my teens I fancied myself a budding singer/songwriter and wrote over a hundred songs (both words and music) before realizing I was a better writer than a singer and gave up my aspirations of joining a band. The urge to rhyme simply transferred to poetry and I've been answering the call ever since.

Unfortunately, the art of the rhyme—something that was

once revered in classic literature—has fallen out of favor, and the publishing opportunities are few and far between. Except in the horror genre. Like some undead beast, horror has kept the rhyme alive. Perhaps dark imagery lends itself naturally to meter and rhyme. Horror is, after all, rooted in the emotions both viscerally and psychologically. It can be a seething, heaving ocean of romanticism or a climbing, diving rollercoaster thrill ride. There's a certain beat to dark poetry that, perhaps, matches the rhythm of the heart.

Novels, short stories, flash fiction, poetry—all have their challenges, but the most rewarding challenge I find, as a writer, is to be able to complete a poetic piece that also rhymes. It's not a trick but a skill. The trick is to make it sound natural, and therein lies the skill. A well-rhymed poem possesses a certain charm. It's no wonder that witches and magician's used metered rhyme to lend power to their incantations. It's as old, as they say, as the hills.

So, don't let anyone tell you that rhyming is for kindergarteners. In every kindergartener is a budding wordsmith. Some will grow up to be rockstars. And some will be satisfied just being a poet.

Kurt Newton

Woodstock Valley, CT

20 March 2022

KURT NEWTON is the author of nine collections of poetry. His dark verse has appeared in the pages of *Weird Tales, Spectral Realms and Cosmic Horror Monthly*, and in the anthologies *Untimely Frost, Death's Garden, Darkling's Beasts and Brews, Putrescent Poems, Burning Love & Bleeding Hearts, Infected,* and *Trickster's Treats 4.*

His Facebook address is **facebook.com/kurt.newton.56**

THE RAVENS QUOTH PRESS is a boutique publisher based in Australia, dedicated to showcasing the best of international poetry craft in beautifully presented publications.

Follow us: **linktr.ee/TheRavensQuothPress**

Lightning Source UK Ltd.
Milton Keynes UK
UKHW022216270622
405049UK00012B/238/J

9 780645 469721